Dead Before Midnight

Pamela Pollack and Meg Belviso

Series Editor: Rob Waring
Story Editor: Julian Thomlinson
Series Development Editor: Sue Leather

HEINLE
CENGAGE Learning

Australia • Bra... ...n • United States

HEINLE
CENGAGE Learning·

Page Turners Reading Library

Dead Before Midnight

Pamela Pollack and Meg Belviso

Publisher: Andrew Robinson

Executive Editor: Sean Bermingham

Senior Development Editor:
Derek Mackrell

Assistant Editor: Sarah Tan

Director of Global Marketing:
Ian Martin

Content Project Manager:
Tan Jin Hock

Print Buyer:
Susan Spencer

Layout Design and Illustrations:
Redbean Design Pte Ltd

Cover Illustration: Eric Foenander

Photo Credits:
61 Wikimedia Commons

ISBN-13: 978-1-4240-1841-3

ISBN-10: 1-4240-1841-2

Heinle
20 Channel Center Street
Boston, Massachusetts 02210
USA

Cengage Learning is a leading provider of customized learning solutions with office locations around the globe, including Singapore, the United Kingdom, Australia, Mexico, Brazil, and Japan. Locate your local office at:
international.cengage.com/region

Cengage Learning products are represented in Canada by Nelson Education, Ltd.

Visit Heinle online at **elt.heinle.com**

Visit our corporate website at
www.cengage.com

Printed in the United States of America
1 2 3 4 5 6 7 – 14 13 12 11 10

Contents

People in the story 3

Chapter 1   The biggest hit on Broadway 4

Chapter 2   Where's John? 9

Chapter 3   A terrible crash 13

Chapter 4   The man in the dressing room 18

Chapter 5   Working too hard 22

Chapter 6   Dead men don't laugh 27

Chapter 7   It's my show now 32

Chapter 8   "I'll give you a hit" 36

Chapter 9   Opening night 41

Chapter 10 Remembered forever 45

Chapter 11 Raymond is waiting 48

Chapter 12 Darkness 52

Review

Chapters 1–4 56

Chapters 5–8 57

Chapters 9–12 58

Answer Key 60

Background Reading

Spotlight on... *Macbeth* 61

Glossary 62

People in the story

David Hawke
a theater director

Lucy Hawke
David's wife, an actress

Scott Savoy
a theater producer

John Mitchell
an older actor

Katie Wright
a young actress

Tad Martin
a young actor

Raymond West
the original writer and
director of the play

This story takes place in New York, in the USA.

Chapter 1

The biggest hit on Broadway

David Hawke ran to the stage of Broadway's Belasco Theater. It was on Forty-Fourth Street in New York. The bright lights of Times Square and the best theaters in the world were nearby. As he passed the empty seats in the theater, David waved a script. He had been reading his copy of the play all night. The script was for the play *Dead Before Midnight* and David was the director.

As he ran through the theater, he couldn't wait to start telling the actors how he wanted to do the play. David jumped up to join the actors on the stage. It was empty except for chairs for the actors. But David had plans to build a set that made the stage look like the inside of a big old house. He could imagine the theater lights hitting the center of the stage when it was all finished. *People would fill every seat in the theater*, he thought. This was David's big chance. He wanted everything to be just right.

When he got up on stage, David kissed his wife, Lucy. She was playing the most important part. Her soft brown hair was pulled back behind her head. She smiled at him and opened her script.

"This play is going to be the biggest hit on Broadway this season," David announced.

The actors smiled at each other.

"It has a lonely country house, a beautiful woman in danger, a killer running after her . . ."

"It's got something else," said John Mitchell. He was an older actor with white hair who had been on Broadway many times. "This play is cursed."

Katie Wright, a young blonde, asked, "What do you mean 'cursed'?"

"They say when people do this play bad things happen," said John. "People die."

"You don't really believe that, do you?" asked Katie.

"Of course not!" a loud voice called from the back of the theater. "There's no danger at all. We're going to make a lot of money!"

Everyone turned their heads. A man in a suit jumped up on the stage. It was Scott Savoy, the producer of the show. "I'm happy to hear you talking about the curse," Scott said. "By opening night I want everyone in the city talking about it."

"What is this curse?" asked Tad Martin, one of the actors.

"It's a great story!" said Scott, stepping in front of David. "Raymond West, the man who wrote the play, killed his leading lady on opening night. Years later someone else—I can't remember his name—put on the play. On opening night he killed his leading lady, too. People say that it's a curse. No one has ever put the play on again—until now!"

"This is so exciting!" said Katie. "My first play on Broadway and it's got its own ghost story! I can't wait to tell everyone."

"That's just what we want to hear," said Scott. "You see, David? I told you this story would make people want to come see the play."

"That's not the only reason for people to come and see the play," David said. "With this cast, how could it not be a hit?"

David took Lucy's hand.

"We won't let you down, Director," said Lucy. "We promise."

"And you have to promise not to kill any of us," said John. "That's what the curse says. David's the director. If the curse is real, he's going to become a killer like Raymond West."

"That's silly, John," said Lucy.

John smiled at the rest of the cast. "Come on, David," he said. "Promise."

David tried to smile back, but he couldn't. When he first heard about the curse he laughed. But now that his dream of directing on Broadway was coming true, he wished he was doing a play that didn't have a curse. Even if the curse was just a story.

"There's no such thing as a curse," said David. "Leave the ghost stories to Scott. We have a show to do. Everyone open your scripts so we can start practice."

They all opened their scripts. On the first page of David's script was a black-and-white photograph of Raymond West. His dark eyes stared out of the page as if they were looking right through David. Raymond West had once been the most famous writer and director in New York, but not as famous as he, David, was going to be. He was right to do the play, whatever scary stories people told about it. This play was just the beginning for David.

Once they started working on the play, no one had time to talk about the curse anymore.

"You're such a good actress," Katie told Lucy one morning when they were practicing. "I want to be as good as you are one day."

"Thanks," said Lucy. "David is a great director. If you listen to him you'll do fine."

She smiled over at David. He was meeting with the men who were going to build the set. He wanted the stage to look like a big house. "I want stairs in the center," he told the men. "Lucy will run up the stairs and disappear." He waved at Lucy.

"Anything you say, David," said the men.

Chapter 2

Where's John?

"OK," said David. "Let's work on the scene with Katie and John again."

Katie played Lucy's friend in the play, and John was the old man who took care of the house. "Katie, get on stage," said David. "Where's John?"

Everyone looked around.

"I didn't see him come back from lunch," said Tad.

David looked at his watch. "That's the third time this week he's been late," he said. "I told him about this. He's . . ."

The door to the theater opened and John came in. "Sorry I'm late," he said, taking off his coat.

David started to walk over to him, but Lucy put her hand on his arm. "Why don't you let me talk to him?" she said. "Actor to actor. Maybe he'll listen to me."

"Give it a try," David said. "He sure doesn't listen to me." He turned back to the stage as Lucy went to talk to John. "Katie, John will be up in a moment."

Lucy and John had a long talk. "He promised to be on time tomorrow," she told David.

"We'll see," he said.

David got to the theater early the next day. To his surprise, John was on time.

David smiled at Lucy when John walked into the theater.

"Looks like he did listen to you," said David, giving her a kiss. "OK," he told everyone, "let's do Katie and John's scene."

John looked around. "Katie isn't here yet."

"Where could she be?" said David. "She's always here by this time."

"I don't mind waiting for her," said John. "I never finished the story I was telling yesterday about that play. The one where I played a horse."

David pulled out his cell phone and called Katie's number. "Where are you?" he asked.

"I'm almost there," Katie said. "I stopped to get some coffee on my way to the theater. John is never there by this time."

"Well, he's here now," David said. "Please get here fast."

David hung up. John was still telling his story. Lucy came to David's side. "I'll talk to Katie when she gets here," she said. "She's a young actress. She should know it's not good to be late."

"She learned that from John," said David. "He's teaching her all the wrong things."

They both looked over at John. He finished his story and everyone laughed.

"John's been in a hundred plays," said David, "and he remembers every single one."

Lucy laughed and said to her husband, "Remember the first play *we* ever did together?"

"How could I forget?" said David. "You were so pretty that every time I tried to talk to you I couldn't speak."

"And I thought you didn't like me," said Lucy. "Because you never spoke to me."

David and Lucy laughed. "It's a good thing we found out the truth," he said, giving her a kiss.

The door to the theater opened and Katie ran in. "Sorry!" she said. "I won't be late again!"

"Just get on stage," David said. "We'll get right to work."

John picked up his script. "Everyone's late sometimes," John said cheerfully.

No, they're not. You're the only one who comes in late, David thought. *It's because of you Katie wasn't on time today.*

David looked at John up on the stage. He would cause more problems if David didn't watch him carefully.

Chapter 3

A terrible crash

David ran up the stairs in the center of the stage. He was running after someone—someone who was going to hurt Lucy. Sweat ran down his face. He was out of breath. He heard a voice laughing.

He reached out for the person. The steps got longer and longer. They disappeared into darkness. They would never end. The person disappeared. Lucy was gone . . . gone . . . gone . . . Who would star in his play?

David sat up in bed, breathing hard.

"That was a really bad dream," Lucy said beside him. "I couldn't wake you up."

David was breathing hard. The dream had felt so real, he wanted to jump out of bed and run after the mysterious person.

"It's the play, isn't it?" said Lucy. "You have to stop worrying so much."

"I can't stop worrying," said David. "I've done a lot of plays, but this one is different. It has to be really good. I can't explain it but I feel like I have to do anything to make this play a hit."

"Being a hit isn't everything," said Lucy. "You've always said what matters is putting on a great show, even if it doesn't make a lot of money. You can't rely on how many people buy tickets to see the show. You just have to know you did a good job."

"I know you're right," said David. "I shouldn't think about all this. But did you hear Scott today talking about how many people are coming to see the show already? If I can be a hit, why shouldn't I be? Why shouldn't we both be a hit?"

David got to the theater early that day. He didn't even wait to walk with Lucy.

There was a scene in the play where Katie discovered a knife stuck in Lucy's picture. The picture was part of the set for the library. The set was pushed out onto the stage by the men who worked at the theater. It came on too slowly, David thought. The people watching the play would have to wait a long time to see it. They would have to wait too long.

One of the men was drinking coffee in the theater when David came in. It was the man's job to move things on the stage during the show.

"I want you to move the set for Katie's scene on faster," David said. "Twice as fast."

The man put down his coffee. "Sorry, Mr. Hawke. That set isn't made to go any faster," he said. "Everything on it could fall over. Someone could get hurt."

"How do you know that if you haven't even tried it?" David said angrily. The man was too lazy, he thought. He didn't want to do extra work to make the play better. Lazy, that was all.

"I know this set," the man said. "I know someone could get hurt if we bring it out too fast."

"I'm the director," said David. "If I tell you to try it, you try it."

The man looked like he was going to say no. Then he waved his hand. "If you say so," he said. "But if something goes wrong . . ."

Lucy came in with Katie. "Get on stage," David told them. "We'll start as soon as John gets here. Where is he?"

"Here I come!" said John, running up to the stage.

They got straight to work. Lucy was playing the character of Jane.

"Miss Jane! Miss Jane!" said Katie. She was playing Jane's friend, Mary. "Come see what's happened in the library!"

Lucy and John ran after her across the stage. This was where the moving set would come on to the stage.

"You see, Miss Jane?" said Katie's character. "Someone has stuck a knife in your picture!"

"Right through the heart," said John.

"Someone is trying to scare me," said Lucy's character. "But I will not be frightened away from this house!"

Lucy looked at John. She waited.

"John!" David called. "You have a line there!"

"Oh yes!" said John. "I forgot."

The set rolled slowly in from stage right. The library set was on it. There was a picture of Lucy with a knife stuck in it, a desk, a chair, and a big clock.

David threw down his script. "That's too slow!" he said. "Study your script, John, while I get one of the men to help."

David went into the wings, on the side of the stage. "Try to move the set again," said David. "Twice as fast. This speed." He walked quickly onto the stage to show them how fast he wanted the set to appear. "Start moving it when Katie says 'Come see what's happened in the library.'"

"But it's not safe," said the man. "Things could fall over if we move it that fast. Did you see how things shook when we pushed it on before?"

"We don't know if they will fall over or not," said David. "That's why we're trying it. Just do it."

David ordered Katie, Lucy, and John to go back to their places. When he had started work on the show, the men who worked on the stage had seemed really helpful. Now he felt as if they just didn't care about the play. Nobody cared about the play the way he did. "Start the scene again!" he shouted.

"Miss Jane! Miss Jane!" said Katie. "Come see what's happened in the library!"

They ran to the right of the stage as the moving set entered from the left. The library set shook, but it was exactly the way David had imagined it. He was right to push the men. They were wrong trying to play it safe. They didn't know that a good play meant taking risks.

"You see, Miss Jane? Someone has stuck a knife in your picture!"

"Right through the heart."

"Someone is trying to scare me," said Lucy. "But I will not be frightened . . ."

"Katie, look out!"

The big clock fell forward. Katie turned around and screamed.

The clock fell with a terrible crash.

Chapter 4

The man in the dressing room

"Katie! Are you all right?"

David jumped up on the stage. Katie was lying next to the broken clock. Lucy was next to her. David went to Katie's side. "That wasn't in the script," he said, taking her hand. His own hand was shaking. Katie could have been killed—all because David had forced the men to do something they said was not safe. David had never had an accident in all the plays he'd done. He had always been careful about the safety of the actors. How could he have done this?

"That was scary," said Katie. "It almost hit me."

"You could have been killed!" said John. "It's a warning." He raised his arms like a ghost. "If we go on with the play, bad things will happen."

"Very funny," said Katie.

"It wasn't a curse that made the clock fall!" David said. "It was my idea. I shouldn't have made them bring the set out so fast."

Lucy put her arm around Katie. "You didn't get hurt, did you?"

Katie shook her head. "No," she said. "I'm OK."

"Maybe we should take a short break," said David. "Everyone be back here in ten minutes. We'll do the scene again."

"Let's go to the dressing room," said Lucy. "I'll make some tea."

Katie left the stage. Lucy went after her. As she went past David, she said, "Everything's OK. She didn't get hurt. It was an accident."

"I told the men to push the set on faster," said David, taking her hand. "I knew it could be dangerous, but I did it anyway. All I cared about was how good it would look on stage." He shook his head. "I just need to be by myself for a little while."

He left the stage and walked through the halls of the theater alone. He still couldn't believe what he had done. He wasn't acting like himself. What if something had happened to Katie? What if she had been hurt?

He opened a door and entered a room where the actors would get ready for the show. There was a long table with chairs in front of it. The actors would sit here to do their makeup. There was a long mirror where they could see themselves. David turned on the lights around the mirror. He sat down in one of the empty chairs.

Lucy isn't angry at me, he thought. Maybe she was right. Accidents happened. He was just trying to do what was best for the show. Katie hadn't been hurt. She was just scared.

David's cell phone rang. "Hello?"

"David? It's Scott. I had to call and tell you. The *New York Star* newspaper wants to do a story about you and Lucy and the play. You're Broadway's most famous couple. Everyone's already talking about *Dead Before Midnight*. They say it's going to be the biggest hit of this year."

"Really?" said David. "A big story? With pictures?"

"Sure!" said Scott.

"Tell the newspaper I'm ready to talk to them whenever they want," said David.

David hung up the phone and looked down at the wooden table. So many actors had sat at this table, getting ready for so many shows. But this show could be bigger than all of them. How could a little accident on the stage have seemed so scary? It was silly for him to worry about Katie.

David lifted his head and looked into the mirror on the wall in front of him. He opened his eyes wide as he looked into the mirror. The man looking back at him from the mirror was a stranger. Instead of David's short hair, he had dark long hair and hair on his face. His black eyes burned into David's.

David had seen this man before. Where had it been? Then he remembered: It was in his script. There was a picture of the man who wrote the play. "You're Raymond West," David said.

Raymond stared back at him.

David didn't believe in ghosts. He had to be seeing things. As he stared into Raymond's eyes in the mirror, Raymond West spoke: "You will put on my play as it was meant to be. *You must not let anything stand in your way.*"

"David?" Lucy said from the door.

David turned around. "What?"

"I heard you talking to someone," she said. "Are you all right?"

David looked back into the mirror. His own face looked out at him where a moment before there had been a different face. Now he looked the same as always. Except for his eyes. David's eyes were blue.

Now they looked dark brown. As dark as Raymond West's eyes.

"I'm fine," David said. "I thought I saw something . . . It was nothing. Everything's all right."

Chapter 5

Working too hard

David asked the actors to come to the theater every day. They worked late into the night. David and Lucy had no time to talk to each other except when they were at the theater. But still David felt as if he should be doing more. If he didn't work harder, the play would fail. They all needed to work harder.

"Katie, do that line again," David said one afternoon. "You don't sound frightened enough when you're calling for John."

Katie sat down. "I've done it fifty times. I don't feel scared. I don't feel anything. I only feel hungry. When's lunch?"

"Lunch is when I say it is," David said.

"David!" said Lucy.

"I think we're all hungry," said John. "It's time for lunch."

"You're eating every time I look at you," said David. "I can't hear your lines when your mouth is full."

John's face went red.

"You can't make me work all day," said Katie. "I'll leave the play."

"You can't . . ." said David.

"Yes, I can," she said. "And I will."

David ran a hand through his hair. "OK, fine. Nobody's working anyway. Everyone can take lunch."

The actors went off the stage, not looking at him. Only Lucy stayed with David.

"How is this play ever going to be ready if all people want to do is eat?" said David.

"What?" said Lucy. "David, listen to yourself. You're angry that people want to eat lunch? Just because you've stopped eating doesn't mean we should stop eating. You're getting thin. And look at your hair." She reached up gently and touched his hair. "It's so long. You should get it cut."

David touched the ends of his hair. It had gotten long. It was almost as long as Raymond West's. He didn't have time to get a haircut. He walked over to a mirror that was part of Lucy's bedroom set. His eyes still looked deep brown. The more he stared at himself the more he saw Raymond West's face.

Lucy appeared behind him in the mirror. "What's the matter?"

"How do I look to you?" he asked her.

"You look like a man who's been working too hard," she said.

She can't see it, David thought. *She doesn't think I look like Raymond West. I'm seeing things. I must be.*

"I'm worried about the show," he said. "John still hasn't learned all his lines. And Scott told me I have three people to talk to on television tomorrow. When I'm talking to them I won't be here to get the play ready."

"I know," said Lucy. "But you can't treat everyone this way. You're not acting like yourself."

"How should I act?" said David. He left the stage and picked up his bag that was lying on a chair. "We've only

got a week until opening night. I don't have the time to fight with Katie or John. They've already cost us too much time."

"Is working on the play all that you care about?" said Lucy.

David pulled some papers out of his bag. He looked through the notes he had made that day. "You know how important this is to me," said David. "The play comes first."

"Before the actors?" said Lucy. "Before people who love you? Before me?"

David looked up in surprise. "What are you talking about?" he said. "Of course I care about you. You're the star. You understand how important this play is to me."

"Is that the only way you care about me?" said Lucy. "As the star of your play? Don't you care about me as your wife?"

David didn't know what to say. Did Lucy really think he didn't care about her? He was doing this play for both of them.

Lucy put her hand on his arm. "David, this play is changing you."

"Of course it's changing me," said David. "It's changing me into the man I always dreamed I'd be. The most important director on Broadway. The one everyone is talking about."

"I didn't marry the most important director on Broadway!" said Lucy. "I care about you, David. Not how famous you are. After opening night, I think you should go away for a while. Get some rest. You need it."

David couldn't believe what he'd just heard. Take a break? Leave New York now? How could Lucy want to take this away from him? How could she do that to him? Didn't she care about him at all?

"Maybe you aren't ready for the play," said David. He turned his back on her. He didn't want to talk about this anymore.

Chapter 6

Dead men don't laugh

David walked up and down in the theater. Lucy waited on the stage. "I'm sure John will be here any minute," she said.

David's cell phone rang. "John?" said David. "We've been waiting for you for half an hour!"

"I can't get out of bed," said John. "I went running last night. I hurt my foot. I can't come in today."

"Well . . . be here on time tomorrow," said David. He hung up the phone. "John's not coming in," he told everyone. *I waited until today to work on this scene because he wasn't ready,* he thought angrily. *Now he's not here.*

Tad was looking at his script. "You can do the scene with me, David," said Tad. "I've been studying my script. If John ever misses a show, I want to be ready to go on."

"That's a good idea," said David. He waved Tad up to the stage.

Tad had been listening carefully when David told John what to do. He knew what David wanted. They went through the scene three times. Each time it got better.

"One more time and I think we've got it," David said. "Try it from Lucy's line about the rope that's missing."

Lucy took her place.

"You must have lost the rope, Carl," Lucy said. "You forgot where you put it. That much rope doesn't just disappear on its own."

"Don't speak about rope in the hanged man's house."

"That line was perfect, Tad!" said David, thinking *John never gets that line right.* "Everyone break for lunch!"

"Thank you, David," said Katie. "That was great, Tad."

"It sure was," David agreed.

Lucy came down off the stage. "See, we got a lot of work done even without John being here."

"More than when John is here," said David.

Lucy put her hand on David's back. "John would do better if you were a little more encouraging," she said. "The way you used to be."

"The way I used to be?" said David. "I was a director of little plays that didn't make any money. This is Broadway. I have to push these people."

Lucy threw up her hands. "I'm going to get some lunch," she said. "I won't ask you to come. I can't remember the last time you took a break for lunch. All you think about is this play. I'm beginning to think it was a mistake to put it on. Maybe that curse is real."

David watched her put on her coat. "Lucy . . ." he said.

"I'll see you after lunch," she said. The door shut behind Lucy, leaving David alone in the theater. He spent his lunch break choosing the best place for John to hang in his death scene.

John came back to the theater the next day. The men who worked on the stage had made his harness for the fourth act of the play. The harness was very strong. It held John up above the stage. He had a rope around his neck, but the harness held him up so that he wasn't hurt. When Lucy discovered him on the stairs she screamed that he had been murdered. The killer was one step closer to her.

Scott was in the theater, too. He had come to see how the harness worked and to tell David about all the people who were going to be at opening night.

"John," David said when they'd done his scene a few times. "You're not getting into place quickly enough."

"It's hard to fit in this harness," John said. "I feel silly."

Everyone laughed except David.

"John, you have time. You have to be dead when Lucy comes on stage. Try it again."

The next time was quicker, but John was laughing.

"Dead men don't laugh," David said. "Try it once more."

Once again Lucy played her scene with Katie. She walked to the middle of the stage. The set turned to reveal John hanging above the stairs.

"That's it!" David said. "You really look dead, John."

John didn't move.

"John?" David said. "John, stop fooling around."

Lucy looked up at John's face.

"Cut him down!" she said.

Two men ran up with a sharp knife. One of them cut through the thick rope.

"Is he breathing?" Lucy asked.

"How could this have happened?" David said. "Maybe he didn't get into the harness right."

"Hurry!" said Katie.

Scott jumped up on the stage. "Get him down right now!" he said.

"Almost!" said the man. "There!"

He cut through the rope and lowered John's body to the second man waiting below with Tad. They laid John out on the floor. His eyes were closed. He didn't move.

Chapter 7

It's my show now

David pulled out his cell phone and called for help. "Help is on its way," he said when he closed the phone.

John lay on the floor. He looked as dead as his character in the play was supposed to be.

A few moments later, two men from the hospital ran into the theater and straight to John.

"He's still breathing," one of them said. "He'll be OK."

"Let's get him to the hospital," said the other.

"We should go with him," Katie said. She was crying.

"That was really scary," said Tad.

"He's got to be OK," said Scott. "He has to be in the show."

Lucy put on her coat. "We should all be there when John wakes up. None of us can work on the play until we're sure he's all right."

"You go ahead," said David.

"Aren't you coming?" asked Lucy.

"I'll follow you," said David. "I have to take care of things here first."

"But what's more important than John?" said Katie.

"I told you I'll follow you," said David. "Go ahead."

"Come on, Scott," said Lucy. "Leave him." They walked out with the rest of the actors.

Left alone, David picked up the broken harness. *Yes,* he thought, *John put it on wrong. That's why he got hurt. We'll have to replace this. John will probably miss another day of work.* David preferred working with Tad anyway. Tad followed his directions and learned his lines. John was better known, but Tad was the better actor.

Wait. What was he thinking? John had almost been killed just now, and David was only thinking about what was best for the play. *Don't I care that John almost died?* David thought. *Did I just want to get John out of the play?*

"Of course you did," said a mysterious voice. "Then Tad could take over the role."

David turned around. "Who said that?" The theater was empty. He looked across the stage. "Who's there?"

Someone stepped out onto the stage. He had the same face and black eyes that David had seen in the dressing room mirror. It was Raymond West.

"You're right, David," Raymond went on. "The play would be better without John. The play is all that matters. You could be the biggest director in New York. Or you could fail. Which do you want?"

David shut his eyes and opened them again. Raymond was still there. When David had seen him in the mirror, he thought he was seeing things. Could he really be a ghost? Could that explain the way he had been acting? Could the curse be real?

The ghost of Raymond West did not move.

"You're dead," David said. "I'm just imagining you're there because I'm worried about the play."

The ghost was still there.

"You're not going to scare me into giving up," said David.

Raymond smiled, almost as if he approved of David. Then he stepped back into the darkness.

"Do you hear me?" David called after him. "This is my show now, Raymond West."

"David!"

David turned around. Lucy had come back into the theater. She looked frightened. "What's the matter? Who are you talking to?"

"Nobody!" said David. "I was just . . . I was talking to myself. Nothing's the matter. I'm fine."

Lucy walked out slowly. "You're not fine, David. You're not fine at all."

Chapter 8

"I'll give you a hit"

John came back to the theater two days later. He and Scott came in together, talking and laughing. "I hope you get a good story in the newspapers out of what happened," said John. "If I'm going to almost die I want my name in the newspaper."

"It's in every paper," said Scott. "Every newspaper in town is running the story and the TV news, too. I made sure of it. Everyone is talking about the play."

"Come here, John," said David. "I bought a new harness for your death scene."

He worked with John very carefully, showing him how to get into it.

"Guess I'd better try it again," said John as he put it over his head.

Everyone stopped to watch. Lucy looked worried.

"I've already been hit by the curse and I lived to tell about it," said John. He smiled. "Don't worry about me."

"It wasn't the curse that got you hurt," said David. "It was because you didn't put the harness on the right way. There's no such thing as a curse. That's something we tell the newspapers. We want them to write stories about the show. But let's not scare each other with it so close to opening night."

"I hope you're right," Katie said.

"I hope he's right, too," said Lucy.

"Of course he's right," said Tad. "David is always right."

John was still trying to smile, but his face was white and his hand shook.

"David," Lucy said. "John's afraid of going up in the harness again after what happened. We should put this off until . . ."

David waved to the man who pulled up the rope tied around John. Suddenly John rose off the floor. He waved his arms in fear.

"David!" said Lucy. "John wasn't ready!"

"See," David called up to John, "there's nothing to be afraid of. There's no curse. The harness works fine if you put it on right."

John tried to laugh.

"Great," David said. "Now I'll bring you down and we can try it again."

John looked sick.

"Are you sure we shouldn't just change John's death scene?" Lucy asked Scott at the end of the day. "He's really scared of that rope. If he got hurt once it could happen again. It doesn't matter how much he practices. Do we really want to take the risk?"

"There's no risk if he does it right," said David. "People will love that scene. Scott's a good producer. He would never give it up. Right, Scott?"

"The scene's supposed to be scary," said Scott. "I don't see a problem. Besides, I already told people about it. They can't wait to see it."

"We don't want them to miss it," said David. "Everyone will remember this scene. John will do fine. Scott, you provide the money, I'll provide the hit."

Over the next few days David timed John over and over until he could get into his harness quickly.

Lucy didn't speak to David much. She talked a lot to Scott, but David didn't know what they were saying.

◇◇◇

"I asked for some last minute changes on Lucy's dress for the third act," David told Lucy and Scott two days before the play opened. "She'll stand out better on stage with a brighter color. I want everyone to look at her."

"Thank you, David," Lucy said. She looked at him carefully. "You look tired. You were up really late last night."

"I'll be up late again tonight," said David. "I won't sleep until after the opening! This is going to be huge!"

"Yeah," Scott said. "The biggest play of the year."

Just that morning David was on a TV show talking about the play. He remembered a man on the TV show asking him if he thought people would like the play. David had looked into the camera and said, "They will never forget it."

Right after he said it, he saw a man across the stage. A man with long hair and brown eyes. For a second he thought it was Raymond West. But when he walked over to the man after the show, he realized he had been looking at his own reflection in a mirror.

The next two days went quickly. David was at the theater late every night. He had only a little time to sleep before returning the next day. On the day of the opening, there

BROADWAY'S STAR COUPLE

was a big story in the newspaper about the play with a picture of David and Lucy. The story called them "Broadway's Star Couple." In the story David said, "I never could have done this without Lucy. This part was made for her. I'm going to make her a star."

David cut the story out of the paper and hung it on the wall in the theater. The actors saw it when they came in. "What a great story!" Katie said. "Lucy's a lucky woman!"

Chapter 9

Opening night

This was it. All David's hard work was for this night. Everyone would see the play. If they loved it, David would be the best director on Broadway. If they didn't like it . . . David didn't want to think about that.

David walked back to the dressing rooms. Everyone was getting ready. He heard John saying his lines. "Don't speak about . . ." he said. "Don't speak about . . ."

David put his head into John's dressing room. "Don't speak about rope in the hanged man's house!" he said. "Have you forgotten your line?"

John laughed. "I won't forget on stage," he said.

David shut the door.

Katie ran up to him. "David, how can I go on stage? I can't do it. I can't go out there."

"Katie, it's OK," said David. He took her by the shoulders. "Breathe deeply. Don't be scared. You'll be fine."

"But I really am scared," she said.

"I'll tell you a secret," said David. "So am I."

Lucy's door was closed. He knew Lucy was ready to go on. He could always trust Lucy.

David went out into the theater. It was already packed with men in suits and women in dresses. David stood in the back. He recognized important writers who would all do reviews of the show in the papers and on TV. He saw famous television and movie stars, all there to see his play.

David knew the play was great, but what if something went wrong? It would be in all the papers. People would laugh at him. David took a deep breath as the lights came down.

Everyone was quiet.

Lucy came on stage. David watched the people around him. Were they scared? Excited? Interested? David couldn't tell.

Katie came onto the stage.

"Miss Jane! Miss Jane!" said Katie. "Come see what's happened in the library!"

David looked over to the side of the stage where the library set came on. Was the grandfather clock shaking? It had worked when they practiced the scene, but what if it fell again now?

David held his breath while the set came on stage.

"You see, Miss Jane? Someone has stuck a knife in your picture!"

"Right through the heart."

"Someone is trying to scare me," said Lucy's character. "But I will not be frightened . . ."

David let out the breath he was holding. The scene was good. Nothing was going to go wrong.

The murderer appeared halfway through the play. Lucy picked up a light. She didn't see the man behind the door. But the people watching the play did. Now it was everyone else's turn to hold their breath. Everything was silent.

Lucy walked up to a window. A big man appeared in the darkness. Lots of people screamed.

David smiled. He knew when a play was working.

When the play stopped after the first half, everyone talked to each other. David listened to them.

"David Hawke has never done anything on Broadway before," said a man David recognized as a writer for the News. "But he's great!"

"I saw him on TV yesterday," said another man, this one from a different newspaper. "He said nobody would forget this play. I didn't believe him then, but he's right."

"I didn't think he could do this play," said the first man, "but he really proved me wrong."

Yes I did, thought David. *If there ever was a curse, I've broken it!*

Chapter 10

Remembered forever

David ran back to see the actors. "Everyone loves it!" he said, running into Lucy's dressing room. It was filled with flowers. People sent them to her for good luck. "I told you we could do it!"

Lucy held him tight. She was still in her clothes from the show. "I'm so happy this went well." She looked him in the eyes. "You know I love you."

"Yes," said David. "And I love you. That's why I want this play to be a hit for us. This show's going to run for years!"

David walked around the room. "I saw a lot of writers outside. We're going to be in every paper and on TV tomorrow. I knew the play would be good, but this is going to make history. We'll be remembered forever. Even longer than Raymond West."

"You don't want to be remembered like him," said Lucy. "He was a murderer."

"He was a great writer and a director," said David. "There wouldn't be a play without him."

"David," said Lucy. She sounded worried.

David did not let her talk. "I wish Tad was playing John's part. Once John leaves the show I'm going to put Tad in the role. Then I'm going to . . ."

"David," said Lucy. She put her hand on his back. "I was going to wait until after the play to speak to you, but I think you should know." Lucy took a deep breath. "John talked to Scott about the way you've been acting. You won't be the director for much longer."

"What?" said David. "They can't make me leave! I should have known John would do something like this. But he's not the only actor in this play. You can talk to Scott and . . ."

"No, I won't," said Lucy. "I'm sorry, David, but I've seen what this play is doing to you. It's better for you if you get away from it. I'm going to tell Scott you should leave the show."

David felt as if she had hit him in the face "You want to take the play away? I can't believe you would do this to me!"

Lucy raised her face to his. She was crying. "I am doing this for you," she said. "The play is changing you! That story about a curse is real. Look at yourself!" She pushed David to the mirror. "You don't even look like yourself anymore. When I look into your eyes I don't see the man I married. You're becoming a completely different person. A person I don't trust. A person like Raymond West!"

David looked at his reflection: long dark hair, brown eyes that burned into his own. *That's me,* he thought. *I've always looked like that. She just wants me to fail.*

"Don't you see, David?" Lucy said. "The play has to end. You can do another play as the man you really are."

Lucy put her arms around him and cried.

"Don't cry, Lucy," said David. "I know you think this is what's best for me." David looked past her into the mirror. Raymond West's face looked back at him. *She doesn't want what's best for you,* the man in the mirror seemed to say. *She never did.*

David spoke to the man with dark eyes in the mirror. "It's all right," he said. "Everything will be all right."

David would not let Lucy take away his play. He knew what he had to do.

Chapter 11

Raymond is waiting

David could not let Lucy take away *Dead Before Midnight*. She must not speak to Scott. She must not speak to anyone ever again.

David went behind the stage to watch the second half of the play. He didn't feel as if he was alone. Raymond West stood beside him.

"You must make it look like an accident," Raymond said in his ear. "Lucy's death will be sad, but there are other actresses who can play the part."

Raymond was right. No one would take the play away from David after his wife was dead.

On stage, Lucy acted her part. She met the killer. He ran after her. The sound effects were perfect. There was a sound like wind blowing.

Just when it looked like Lucy's character Jane was going to die, she stepped to one side and the killer fell into a space under the ground that was meant for her. Jane pushed a heavy stone over the space. The killer was stuck.

"Oh, Miss Jane!" cried Katie, running on stage. "I thought you were dead for sure!"

"I'm all right, Mary," said Lucy's character. "That man will never hurt me or anyone in my house ever again. Now run and get the police. Someone will have to get him out of there. I can hear him screaming."

Lucy left the stage. The final scene was a small one between Katie and Tad. Tad played a young policeman. Tad moved the stone to arrest the killer and found the space empty. The killer had disappeared.

While Katie and Tad did their scene, David waited for Lucy to come off the stage. "That was perfect," David said, putting his arms around her. "Come on, I want to show you something."

"Now?" said Lucy. "I have to be on stage in a few minutes."

"You'll be on stage," said David. "You know no one cares about the play as much as me."

Lucy looked worried. "David, you're not angry about what I said, are you? I care about you. So does Scott. We want the best for you."

"I understand," said David, taking her to the stairs that led up above the stage. Raymond West was waiting there. David started up the stairs. "I understand everything now," said David. "That's what I want to show you."

"OK," said Lucy. She pulled on his hand. "But I really have to get ready to go back on stage. You can show me later."

"Later will be too late," said David. He took her arm in both his hands and pulled her up the stairs.

"David, stop it!" said Lucy.

She held back, but David knew he was too strong for her. He was stronger than he had ever been. He felt as if he had the strength of two men.

"I'm coming, Raymond!" David called. "I know what I have to do!"

"Raymond?" said Lucy, trying to pull away. "David, Raymond West is dead. There's no one here but us. Whatever you think you have to do . . ."

"I know what I have to do," said David. "I have to save the play. I have to save the play from you!"

Chapter 12

Darkness

David and Lucy were high above the stage.

Raymond stepped out of the darkness. He held out his hand to David.

"David, let me go! You're hurting me!" said Lucy.

"You want to hurt me," said David. "You want Scott to take the play away from me. But I won't let you. You're going to have an accident. Don't worry, things like this happen all the time. The theater is a dangerous place." David laughed. "Maybe Scott will tell the newspapers it's part of the curse."

David pulled Lucy past the big theater lights. Far below, he could hear Katie and Tad doing their last scene. He could see the rope from John's death scene. Lucy was going to die too.

Lucy kicked and fought him. She tried to pull herself out of David's hands. It was easy to hold her. It was as if Raymond was giving him strength.

"David, that's crazy," Lucy said. She started to cry. "People will know I didn't come up here by myself. Everyone will know what you did. You won't ever see a play again. You're just not thinking clearly!"

"Oh, I'm thinking clearly," said David. "Why would anyone believe I wanted to kill you? You're my wife. I would never hurt you. Just like you would never hurt me."

"If she really loved you she would never take away the play," said Raymond to David. "No one will know you killed her."

Below them, Katie and Tad finished their scene.

"Help!" Lucy screamed. "Somebody help me! Up here!"

David heard voices from below.

"Lucy?" called Katie. "Where are you?"

"Do it!" Raymond shouted. "Before they come!"

David reached for Lucy.

"I never tried to hurt you!" Lucy cried. "And you don't really want to hurt me. David, you're not a murderer! I love you and you love me!"

Lucy's voice seemed to wake David, as if from a sleep. He opened and closed his eyes. Was this a dream? Why were he and Lucy high above the stage?

"Kill her!" said Raymond. "Do it now!"

"No!" David said, his eyes open. "I won't do it."

Raymond's black eyes glowed in the darkness.

"Very well," Raymond said. "Then I will."

Raymond moved quickly to push Lucy off the platform.

"Lucy, look out!"

David jumped in front of her. He pushed Raymond away. His hands went right through him. David fell forward.

Lucy screamed. She reached for David. Too late. David fell off the edge of the platform into the darkness.

David fell. Air went past his ears quickly. His head spun.

He heard Lucy calling his name.

Lucy. She was alive. He hadn't killed her. Raymond West had not won. David tried to say her name. He hit the floor. Everything went black.

Daily News

YOUNG DIRECTOR'S DEATH SHOCKS BROADWAY

Opening night ended badly this week when director David Hawke fell to his death after his hit show, *Dead Before Midnight*. Actors in the show agreed that Hawke had been working very hard in the weeks before opening night.

"I had an accident myself just days before," said actor John Mitchell. "I suppose you've heard about the play being cursed. Everyone's talking about it now. We're sold out through the end of the year."

Hawke's wife, Lucy, left the show after her husband's death. "I have nothing to say about what happened that night," she said. "It was just a terrible accident."

Because people loved the play in New York, producers are planning a London production. The new production will be directed by New York cast member John Mitchell.

"It's going to be the biggest hit in London," Mitchell said. "I've been in the theater all my life and can't wait to get to work. I've already started looking for my leading lady. I feel like I'm meant to put on this play."

Asked if he is worried about the curse, Mitchell laughed and said, "Those are just stories. But if Raymond West wants to come after me, he knows where to find me."

Review: Chapters 1–4

A. Match the characters in the story to their descriptions.

1. _____ David Hawke
2. _____ Lucy Hawke
3. _____ Scott Savoy
4. _____ Katie Wright
5. _____ Raymond West
6. _____ John Mitchell
7. _____ Tad Martin

a. theater producer
b. lead actress and David's wife
c. a young actress
d. director of the play
e. an old and experienced actor
f. a young actor
g. the original director of the play

B. Complete the crossword puzzle.

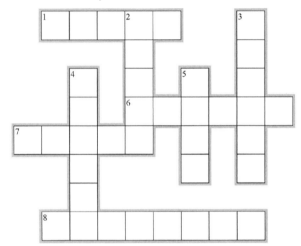

Across

1. A big _____ falls and nearly kills Katie.
6. David dreams he is chasing someone up the _____.
7. In the play, Miss Jane's picture has a _____ stuck in it.
8. The theater area in New York is known as _____.

Down

2. *Dead Before Midnight* is famous for having a _____ on it.
3. David first sees Raymond West in the _____ of his dressing room.
4. Raymond West was the original _____ and director of the play.
5. David thinks the man who moves the set is too _____.

Review: Chapters 5–8

A. Read each statement and circle whether it is true (T) or false (F).

1. David thinks Tad is a better actor than John.   T / F
2. When they first met, Lucy knew that David liked her.   T / F
3. David never has time to eat his lunch during play practice.   T / F
4. John does not come for practice one day because he hurt his foot. T / F
5. Tad gets into an accident and goes to hospital.   T / F

B. Choose the best answer for each question.

1. According to Lucy, how has David changed since they started the play?
   a. He has gained weight.
   b. He sleeps a lot.
   c. He no longer wants to be a director.
   d. He's getting thin and his hair is long.

2. What does David say should come first?
   a. Lucy
   b. the play
   c. the actors
   d. himself

3. Lucy thinks David should _____ after opening night.
   a. start a new play
   b. quit theater forever
   c. become an actor
   d. take a break

4. According to David, what is the main reason for John getting hurt?
   a. He did not put the harness on right.
   b. The play is cursed.
   c. The harness was broken.
   d. The scene is too dangerous.

5. Who is the person with long hair and brown eyes that David sees in the TV studio?
   a. Scott Savoy
   b. Raymond West
   c. his own reflection
   d. a woman with long hair

Review: Chapters 9–12

A. Write the name of the character who said the words.

1. "If she really loved you, she would never take away the play."

_____

2. "When I look into your eyes, I don't see the man I married."

_____

3. "I've already been hit by the curse and I lived to tell about it.
   Don't worry about me."

_____

4. "Every newspaper in town is running the story and the TV news, too.
   I made sure of it."

_____

5. "I knew the play would be good, but this is going to make history.
   We'll be remembered forever."

_____

B. Read each statement and circle whether it is true (T) or false (F).

1. John tells Scott that David should leave the show.   T / F
2. Lucy and David can both see the ghost of Raymond West.   T / F
3. David isn't worried that people will know he has killed Lucy.   T / F
4. Lucy does not tell the newspapers what really happened.   T / F
5. John is going to direct the play in London.   T / F

C. Complete each sentence with the correct word or words from the box.

ticket	wings	script	understudy
cast	dressing room	opening	set

1. _____ night is the first time a play is put on for other people.

2. The _____ is where actors change their clothes.

3. Actors usually wait in the _____ right before they go onstage.

4. People who act in the play are called its _____ .

5. You buy a(n) _____ so you can enter the theater to watch a play.

6. A(n) _____ is the actor who goes on in the place of the usual actor.

7. Actors must learn their lines from the _____ .

8. The space or background built for a play is called a(n) _____ .

Answer Key

Chapters 1–4

A:

1. d; **2.** b; **3.** a; **4.** c; **5.** g; **6.** e; **7.** f

B:

Across

1. clock; **6.** stairs; **7.** knife; **8.** Broadway

Down:

2. curse; **3.** mirror; **4.** writer; **5.** lazy

Chapters 5–8

A:

1. T; **2.** F; **3.** T; **4.** T; **5.** F

B:

1. d; **2.** b; **3.** d; **4.** a; **5.** c

Chapters 9–12

A:

1. Raymond West; **2.** Lucy Hawke; **3.** John Mitchell; **4.** Scott Savoy; **5.** David Hawke

B:

1. F; **2.** F; **3.** T; **4.** T; **5.** T

C:

1. Opening; **2.** dressing room; **3.** wings; **4.** cast; **5.** ticket; **6.** understudy; **7.** script; **8.** set

Background Reading:
Spotlight on . . . *Macbeth*

By the pricking of my thumbs, Something wicked this way comes...
— Macbeth, Act IV, Scene 1

One of the most famous "cursed" plays is William Shakespeare's historical play *Macbeth*.

The three witches from *Macbeth*, by William Rimmer (1816–1879)

Shakespeare wrote *Macbeth* in the early 17th century. The play is set in Scotland, and has a very dark theme, including scenes of fighting, murder, and war.

Many people say the play is unlucky, perhaps even cursed.

- On its opening night—August 7, 1606—the 13-year-old boy playing the role of Lady Macbeth (there were no female actors in those days) got a high fever. He could not perform, so Shakespeare himself had to play the role.
- In a performance in Amsterdam in 1672, the actor playing *Macbeth* walked on with a real dagger. He used it to kill one of the other actors.
- In 1849, 30 people died in a riot during a performance of *Macbeth* at New York's Astor Place Opera House.
- When the English actor Laurence Olivier played *Macbeth* in 1937, his sword broke and flew into the audience, hitting a man in the face. The man later died of a heart attack.

Some actors feel so strongly about *Macbeth*'s curse that they will not say its name. Instead they call it "The Scottish Play." If an actor does say it by accident, they have to leave the theater and turn around three times, shouting loudly. Then they must ask to be let back in!

So, is there really a curse? To believe or not to believe—that is up to you!

Think About It

1. What other reasons could help explain the "curse" of *Macbeth*?
2. Do you know of other curses, or examples of bad luck? Do you believe they are true?

Glossary

Broadway	(*n.*)	a famous street in New York City with many theaters
cast	(*n.*)	the actors in a play
curse	(*n.*)	something that brings bad luck
director	(*n.*)	a person who tells the actors and other people who work on a play what to do
glow	(*v.*)	to light up
harness	(*n.*)	a thing that holds someone up
lines	(*n.*)	the words of an actor's part in a play
mirror	(*n.*)	a glass where you can see your reflection
opening	(*n.*)	the first time a play is put on for people
platform	(*n.*)	a floor high above the ground
rope	(*n.*)	a long, thick string for tying things
script	(*n.*)	the papers that actors learn their lines from
set	(*n.*)	a fake setting built for a play
star	(*n.*)	a well-known actor
theater	(*n.*)	a building where people watch plays
ticket	(*n.*)	a small piece of paper you buy to see a play
Times Square	(*n.*)	a busy area in New York City known for its theaters, restaurants, and bright lights
wings	(*n.*)	the unseen area on either side of a stage